BASS
RECORDED VERSIONS

Transcribed by STEVE GORENBERG

NIRVANA
THE BASS COLLECTION

ISBN 0-7935-7337-8

IMP International Music Publications Limited
Southend Road, Woodford Green, Essex IG8 8HN, England

NIRVANA
THE BASS COLLECTION

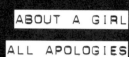
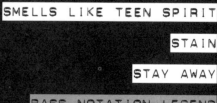
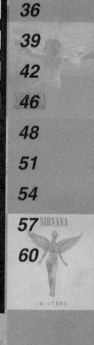

About a Girl

Words and Music by Kurt Cobain

Tune Down 1/2 Step:

①= Gb   ③= Ab

②= Db   ④= Eb

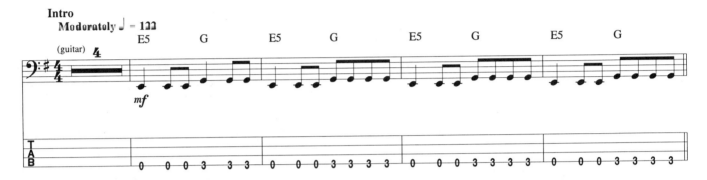

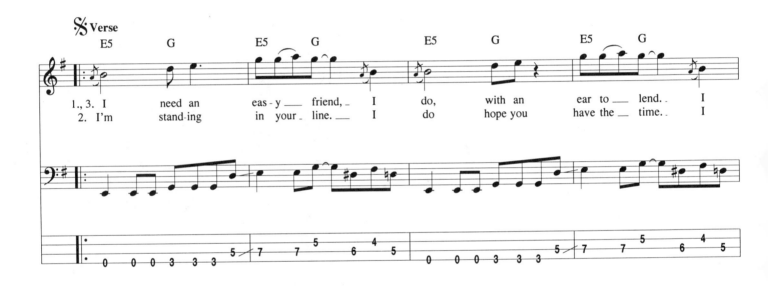

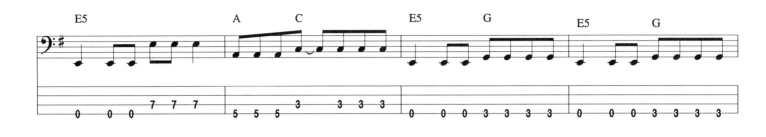

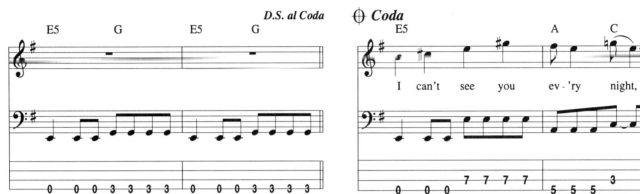

D.S. al Coda   Coda

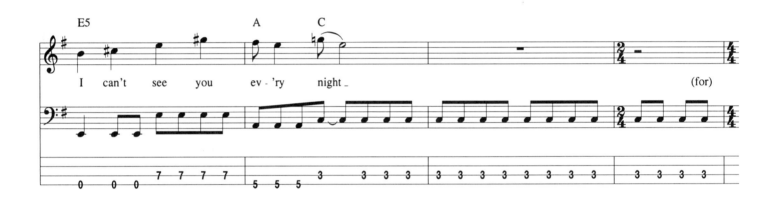

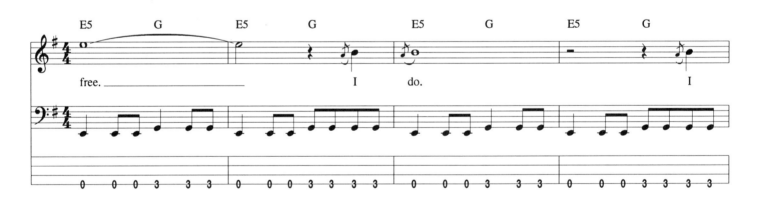

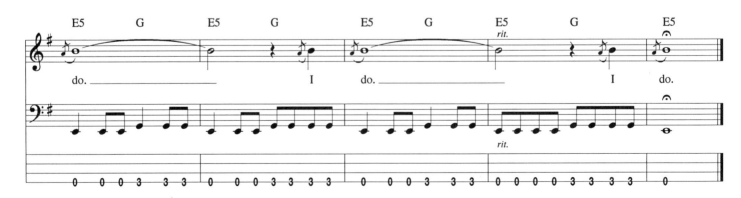

All Apologies

Words and Music by Kurt Cobain

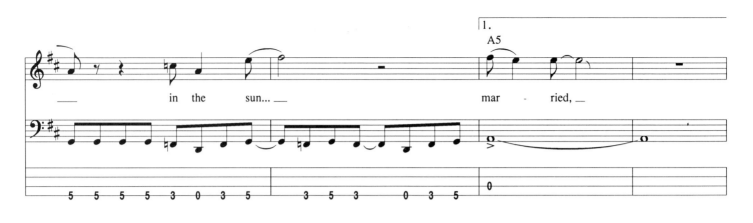

in the sun... mar - ried,

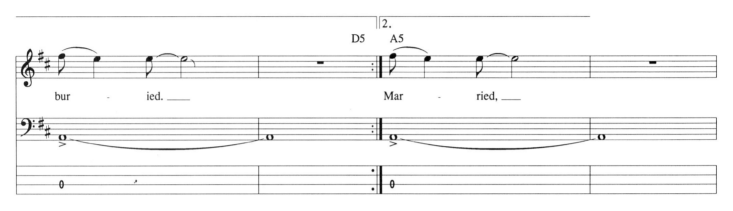

bur - ied. Mar - ried,

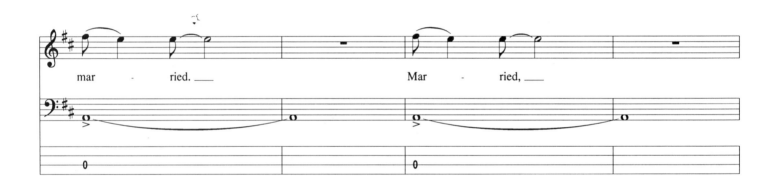

mar - ried. Mar - ried,

Chorus

bur - ied, yeah, yeah, yeah, yeah.

Blew

Words and Music by Kurt Cobain

Tune Down 2 Whole Steps:

② = Eb   ③ = F

① = Bb   ④ = C

Intro

Moderately ♩ = 120

N.C.

(band in)

E5   G5 A5 Bb5   A5   G5   A5   N.C.   G5 A5 Bb5   A5   G5   A5

Bass Fig. 1   End Bass Fig. 1

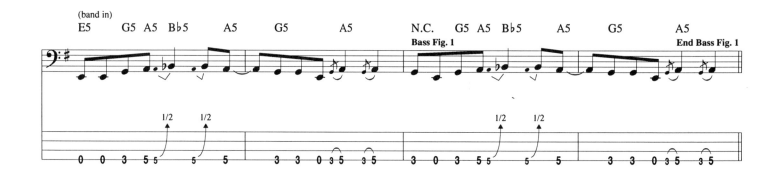

Verse

w/ Bass Fig. 1, 8 times

N.C.(E5)   A7   N.C.(E5)   A7

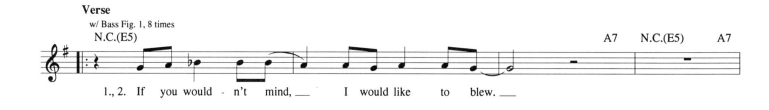

1., 2. If you would - n't mind, ___ I would like to blew. ___

N.C.(E5)   A   N.C.(E5) A7(no3rd)

If you would - n't mind, ___ I would like to lose. ___

If you would-n't care ___ I would like to leave. ___

If you would-n't mind, ___ I would like to breathe. ___

𝄋 Chorus

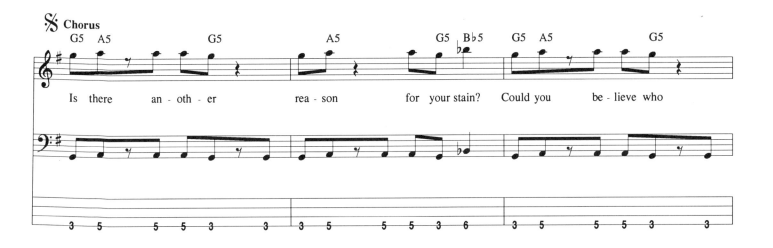

Is there an-oth-er rea-son for your stain? Could you be-lieve who

To Coda ⊕

we knew stress or strain? Here is an-oth-er word that rhymes with shame. ___

Guitar Solo

D.S. al Coda

Coda

N.C.

play 3 times

You could do an - y - thing. __ You could do an - y - thing. __ You could do an - y - thing.

Free Time

E5

You could do an - y - thing. __

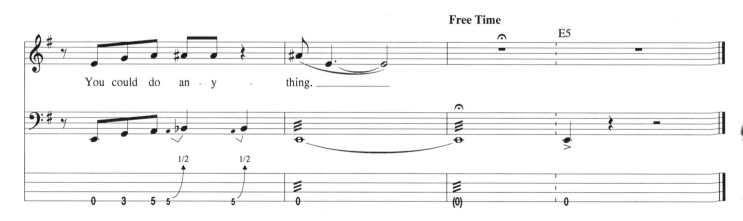

Come As You Are

Words and Music by Kurt Cobain

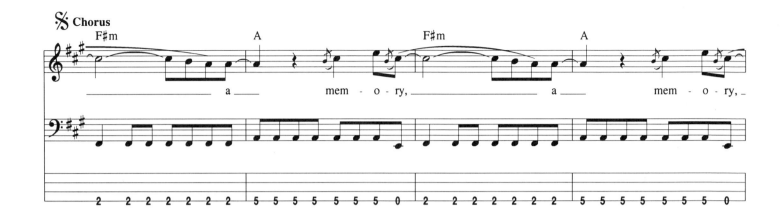

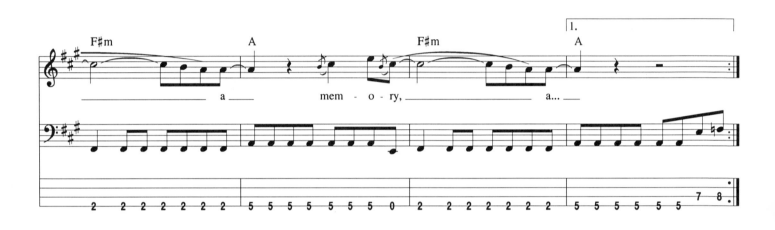

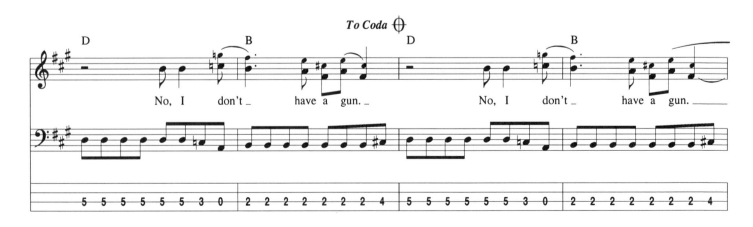

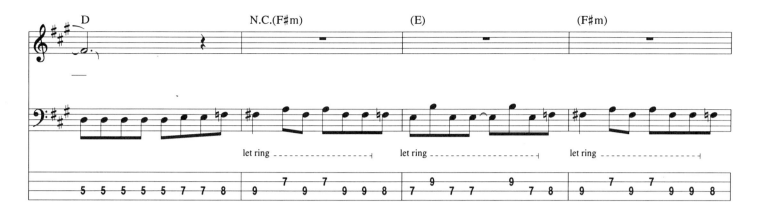

Guitar Solo

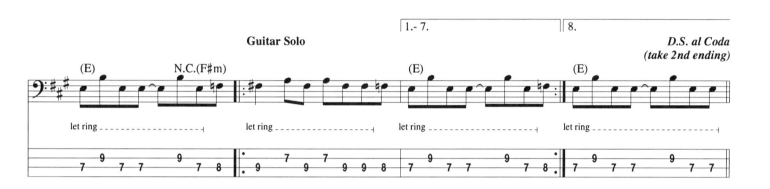

D.S. al Coda
(take 2nd ending)

⊕ *Coda*

No, I don't __ have a gun. __ No, I don't, __

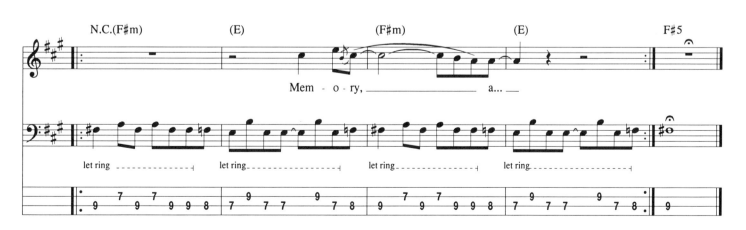

Mem - o - ry, _____ a...

Dumb

Words and Music by Kurt Cobain

Tune Down 1/2 Step:
①=Gb ③=Ab
②=Db ④=Eb

Verse
Moderately ♩ = 114

1, 3. I'm not like them, but I can pretend. The sun is gone, but I have a light.
2. My heart is broke, but I have some glue. Help me in-hale and mend it with you.

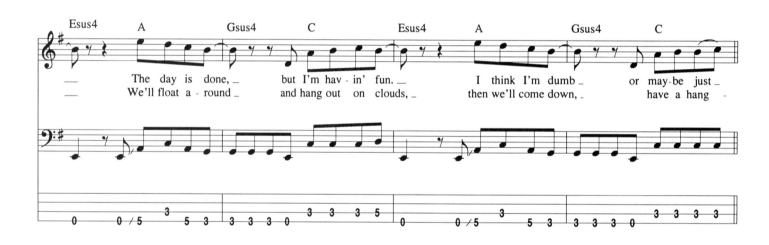

The day is done, but I'm hav-in' fun. I think I'm dumb or may-be just
We'll float a-round and hang out on clouds, then we'll come down, have a hang -

Chorus

hap-py. Think I'm just hap-py.
o-ver. And have a hang - o-ver.

Think I'm just
Have a hang -

Bridge

Coda

Floyd the Barber

Words and Music by Kurt Cobain

Heart Shaped Box

Words and Music by Kurt Cobain

Drop D Tuning, Down 1/2 Step:
① = G♭ ③ = A♭
② = D♭ ④ = D♭

Intro
Moderately ♩ = 100

1., 3. She _ eyes me _ like _ a Pi - ces when _ I _ am weak. _

I've been locked in - side _ your heart - shaped box _ for _ weeks. _

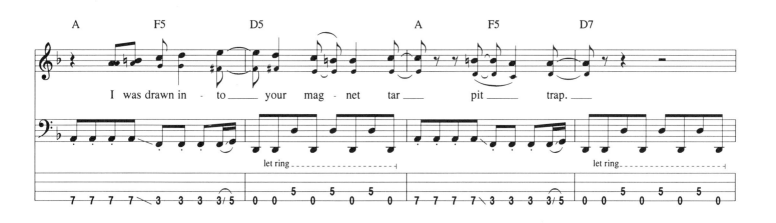

I was drawn in - to ___ your mag - net tar ___ pit ___ trap.

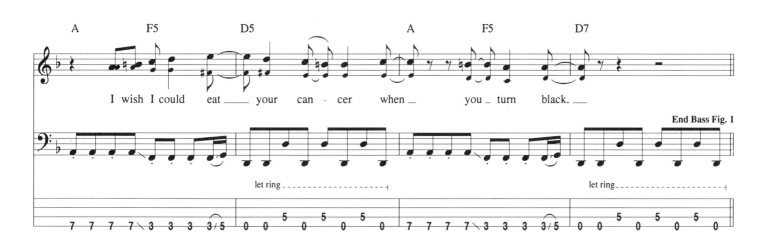

I wish I could eat ___ your can - cer when ___ you ___ turn black. ___

End Bass Fig. 1

Chorus

Hey! Wait! I've got a new com-plaint. For - ev - er in debt ___ to your price - less ad - vice. ___

Bass Fig. 2

w/ Bass Fill 2, 2nd time

___ Hate! Haight! I've got a new com-plaint. For - ev - er in debt ___ to your price - less ad - vice. ___

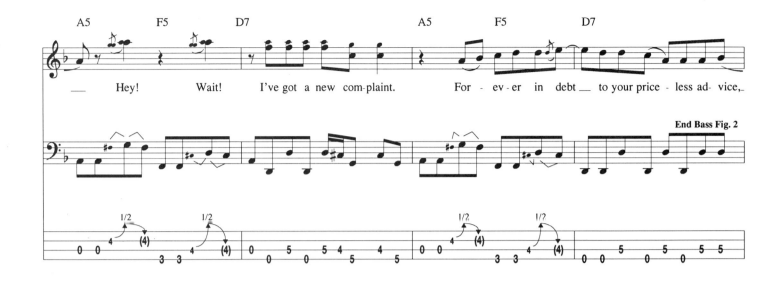

Hey! Wait! I've got a new com-plaint. For-ev-er in debt __ to your price-less ad-vice,

End Bass Fig. 2

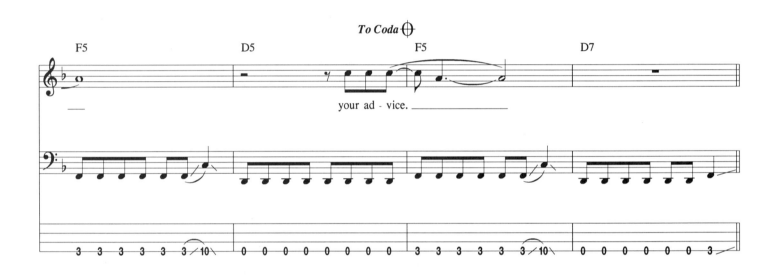

To Coda ⊕

your ad-vice. _____

Verse
w/ Bass Fig. 1

2. Meat-eat-ing or-chids for-give no ___ one ___ just yet. ___

w/ Bass Fill 1

Cut my-self on an-gels hair ___ and ba - by's ___ breath. _

Bass Fill 1

Brok-en hy-men of ___ your high - ness, I'm ___ left ___ black. ___

Throw down your um - bil - i - cal noose ___ so I can climb ___ right back. ___

Chorus
w/ Bass Fig. 2

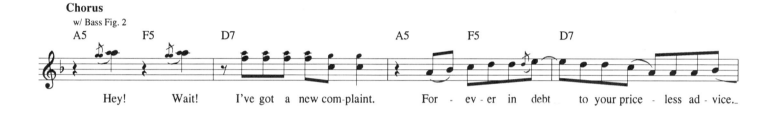

Hey! Wait! I've got a new com-plaint. For - ev - er in debt to your price - less ad - vice. ___

w/ Bass Fill 2

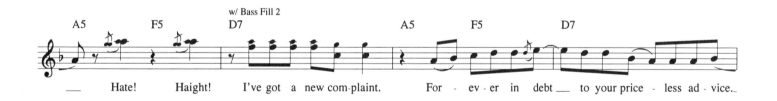

___ Hate! Haight! I've got a new com-plaint. For - ev - er in debt ___ to your price - less ad - vice. ___

___ Hey! Wait! I've got a new com-plaint. For - ev - er in debt ___

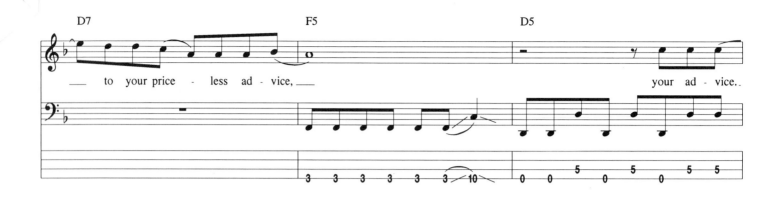

to your price - less ad - vice, ____ your ad - vice. __

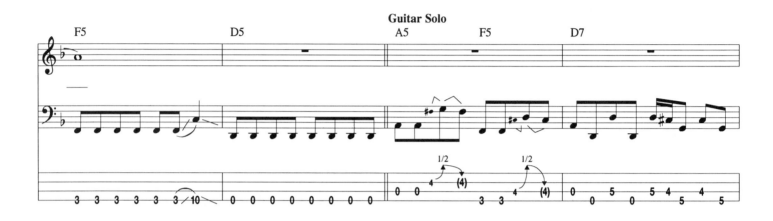

Guitar Solo

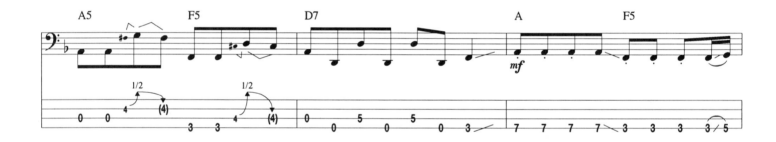

D.S. al Coda

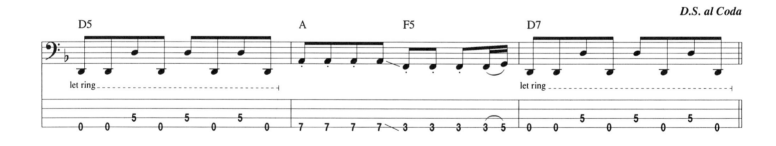

let ring

⊕ *Coda*

1., 2.

3.

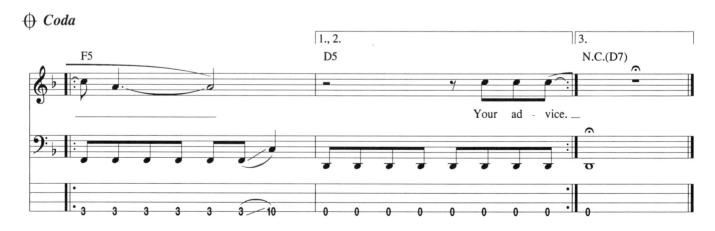

Your ad - vice. __

In Bloom

Words and Music by Kurt Cobain

the one _ who likes   all our pret-ty songs _ and he   likes to sing a-long _ and he   likes to shoot his gun, _ but he

¹ Harmonies sung 3rd time, first six meas. of chorus.

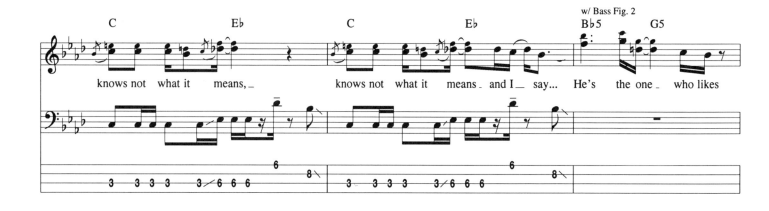

knows not   what it   means, _   knows not   what it   means _ and I _ say... He's   the one _   who likes

all   our pret-ty songs _   and he   likes to sing a-long _   and he   likes to shoot his gun, _   but he

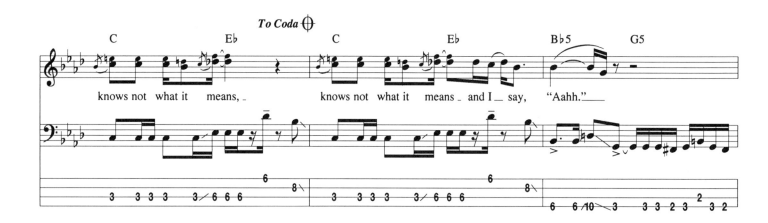

knows what it   means, _   knows not what it   means _ and I _ say,   "Aahh." _

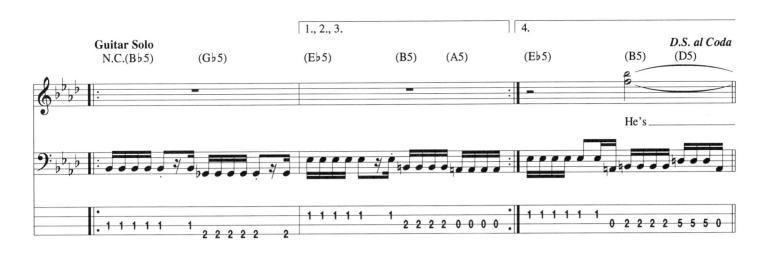

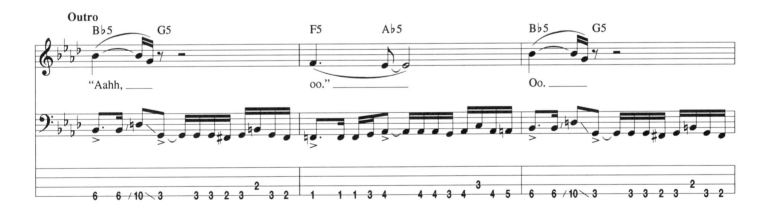

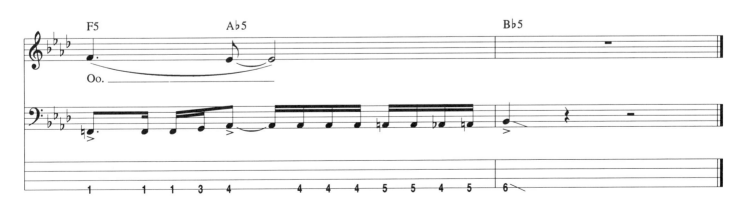

Lithium

Words and Music by Kurt Cobain

Tune Down 1 Whole Step:
①=F ③=G
②=C ④=D

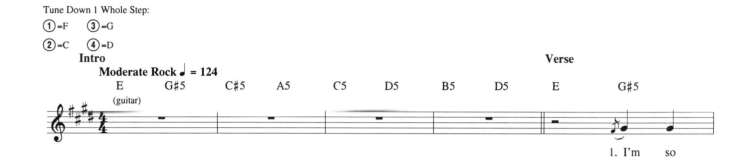

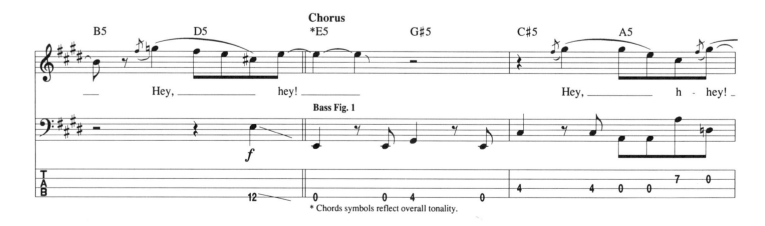

* Chords symbols reflect overall tonality.

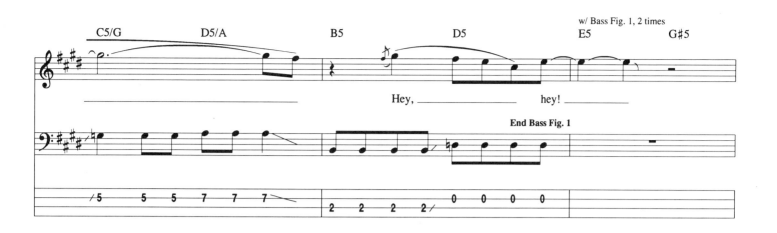

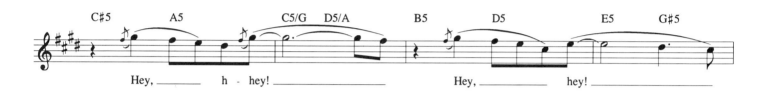

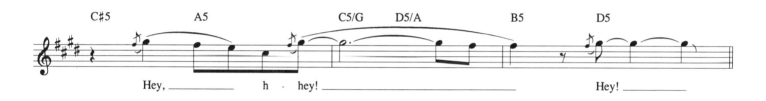

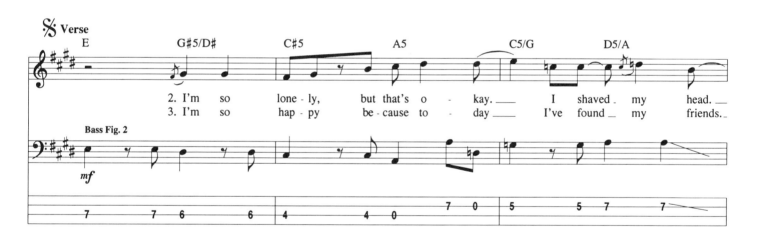

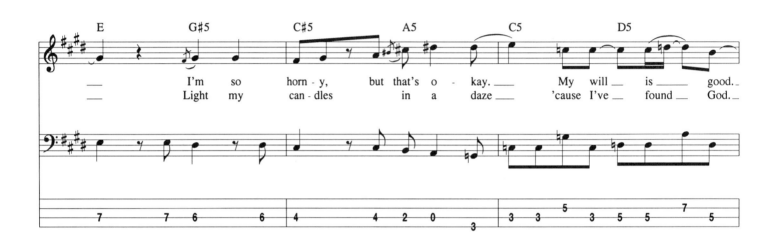

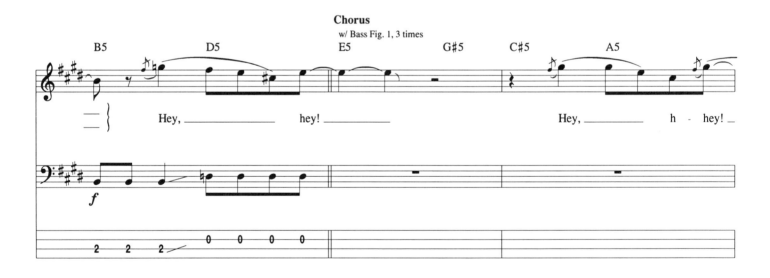

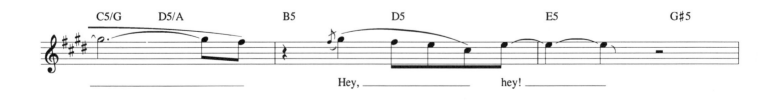

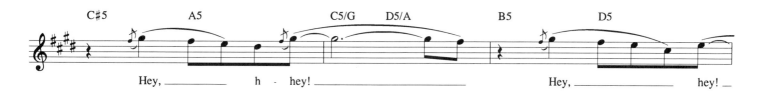

Hey, _____ h - hey! _____ Hey, _____ hey! _____

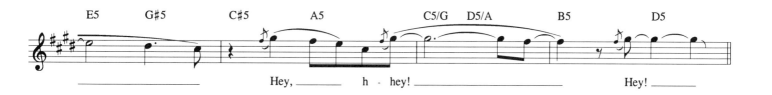

_____ Hey, _____ h - hey! _____ Hey! _____

Bridge

1., 2. I like you, } I'm not gon - na crack. I miss you,
3., 4. I like it, }

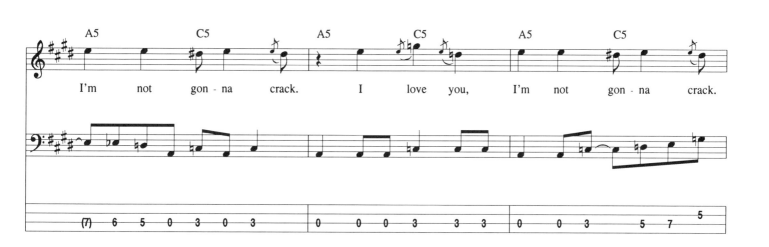

I'm not gon - na crack. I love you, I'm not gon - na crack.

Bass Fill 1

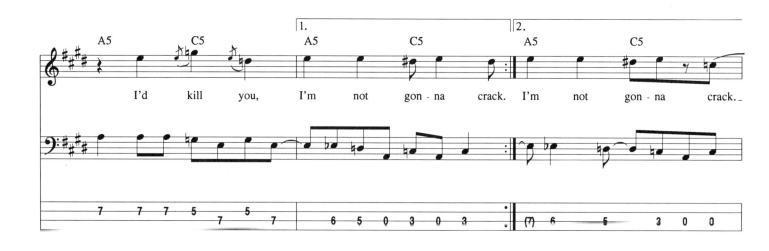

I'd   kill   you,   I'm   not   gon - na   crack.   I'm   not   gon - na   crack.

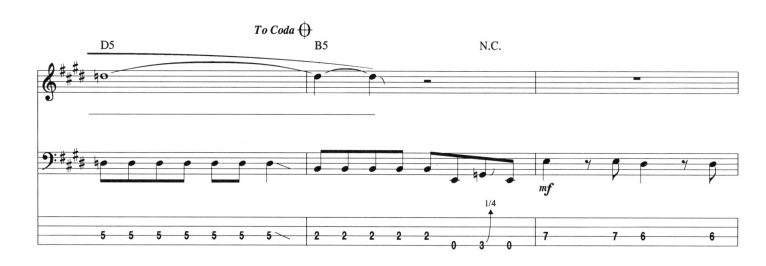

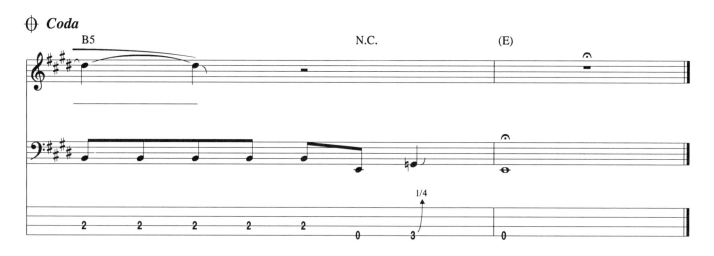

Lounge Act

Words and Music by Kurt Cobain

Verse

* 1., 3. Truth / cov-ered in se-cu-ri-ty, ___ I can't let you smoth-er me. _
2. Don't / tell me what I want to hear. ___ A-fraid of nev-er know-ing fear,_

* Sing 3rd Verse and Chorus *8va.*

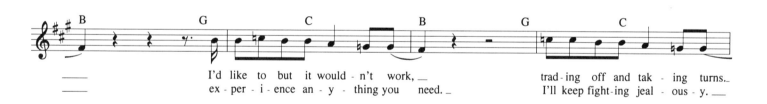

___ I'd like to but it would-n't work, ___ trad-ing off and tak-ing turns._
___ ex-per-i-ence an-y-thing you need. _ I'll keep fight-ing jeal-ous-y._

Chorus

w/ Bass Fill 1, 3rd time (see next page)

___ I don't re-gret a thing. } And I've got ___ this friend, _ you see ___ who makes_ me feel
___ Un-til it's fuck-ing gone. }

33

and I want - ed more ___ than I ___ could steal. I'll ar - rest ___ my - self, ___ I'll wear a shield.

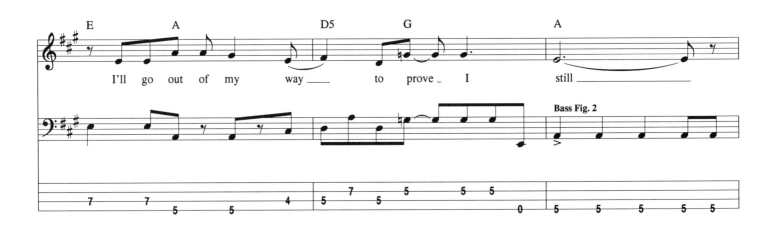

I'll go out of my way ___ to prove __ I still _____

smell her on you. ___

34

$\oplus$ *Coda*

I'll go out __ of my way __ to make __ you a deal. We've made __ a pact __ to learn __ from who-

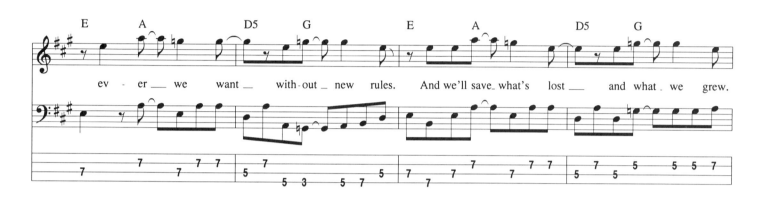

ev- er __ we want __ with-out __ new rules. And we'll save __ what's lost __ and what __ we grew.

w/ Bass Fig. 2, 2 times

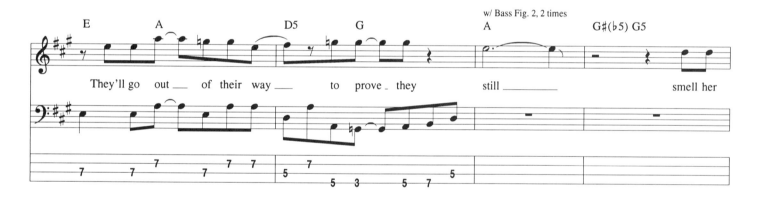

They'll go out __ of their way __ to prove __ they still __ smell her

on you, __ I still __ smell her

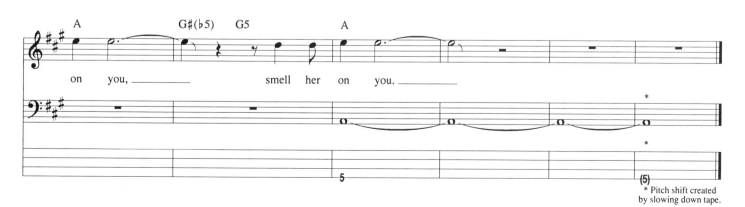

on you, __ smell her on you. __

* Pitch shift created
by slowing down tape.

35

Mr. Moustache

Words and Music by Kurt Cobain

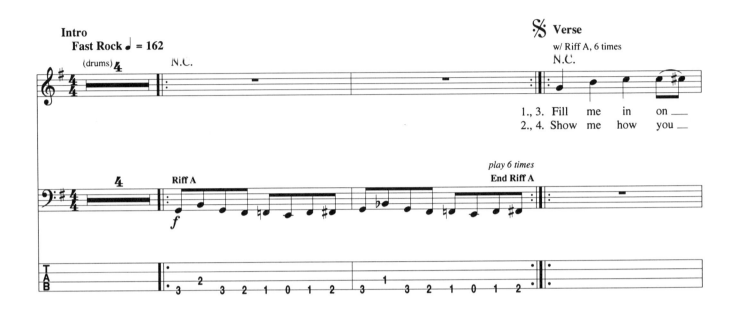

your new vis - ion, wake me up with in - de - cis - ion. Help me trust your
ques - tion ques - tion, lead the way to my temp - ta - tion. Take my hand and

might - y wis - dom, yes, I eat cow, I am not proud. _____
give it clean - ing, yes, I eat cow, I am not proud. _____

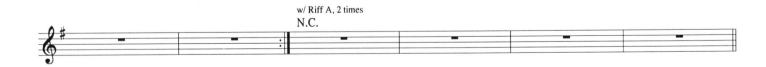

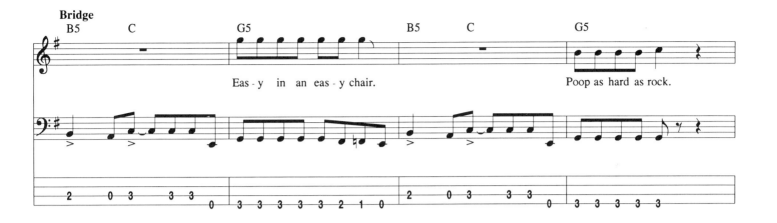

Easy in an easy chair.
Poop as hard as rock.

I don't like you anyway.
Seal it in a box.

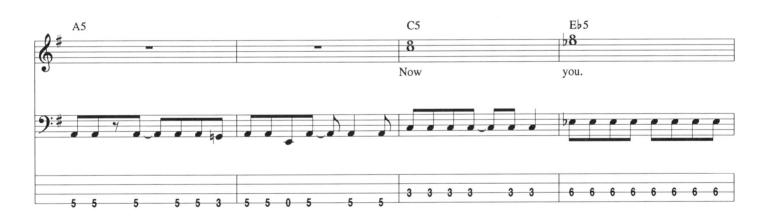

Now you.

Now you.

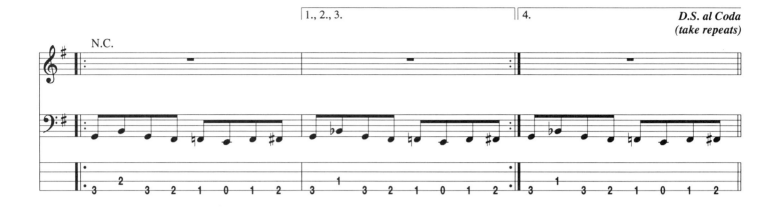

Coda

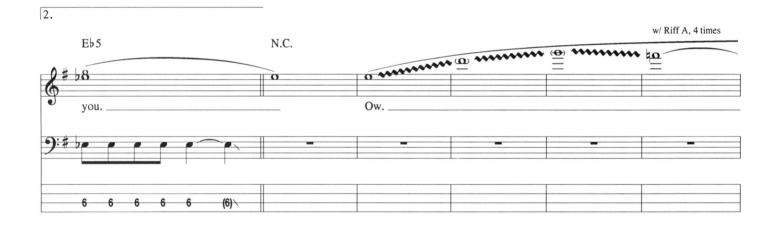

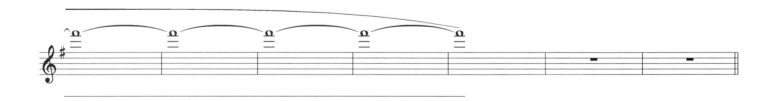

Outro

On a Plain

Words and Music by Kurt Cobain

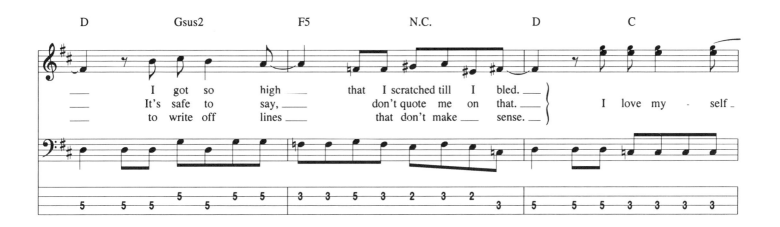

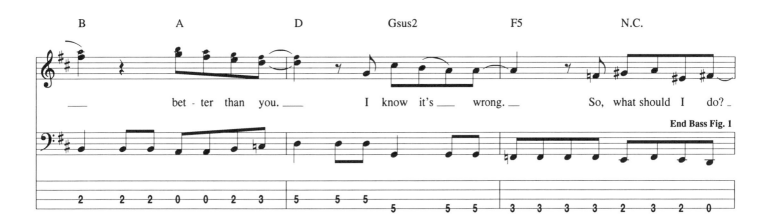

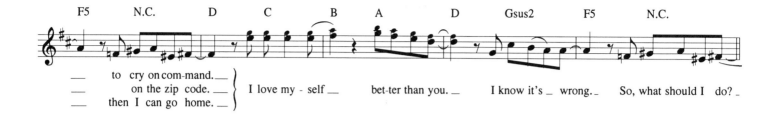

— to cry on com-mand. —
— on the zip code. —
— then I can go home. —
I love my - self — bet-ter than you. — I know it's — wrong. — So, what should I do? —

Chorus
w/ Bkgd. Voc. Fig. 1, 4 times

I'm on a plain. — I can't com-plain. —

I'm on a plain. —

Some - where I have heard — this be - fore,

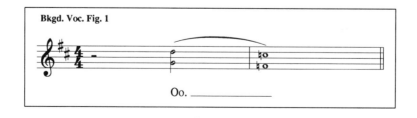

Oo. _____

40

in a dream my mem-'ry has stored.

As de-fense I'm neu-tered and spayed.

D.S. al Coda

What the hell am I try-ing to say? ____

Coda

I can't com-plain. ____ I'm on a plain. I can't com-plain. ____

w/ Bkgd. Voc. Fig. 1, 2 times

* Play 4 Times and Fade

simile on repeats

* Bkgd. vocals do not fade out.

Penny Royal Tea

Words and Music by Kurt Cobain

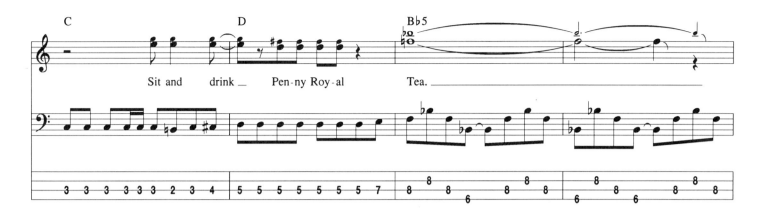

Sit and drink _ Pen-ny Roy-al Tea. _____

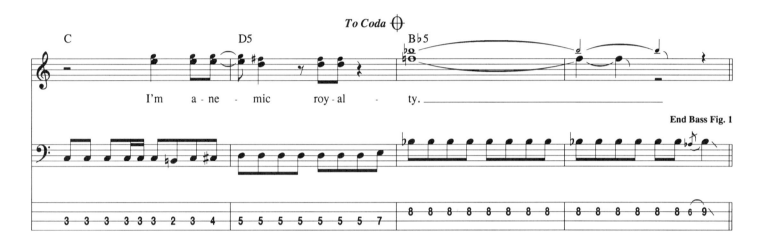

To Coda ⊕

I'm a-ne - mic roy-al - ty. _____

End Bass Fig. 1

Verse

2. Give me a Leo-nard Coh-en af-ter world, _

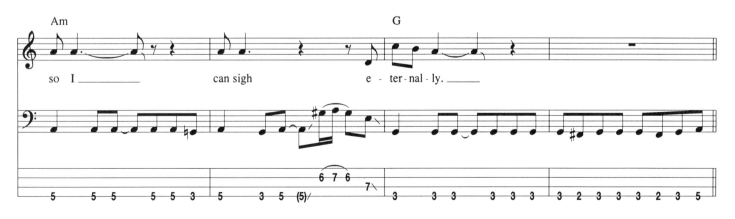

so I _____ can sigh e-ter-nal-ly. _____

Chorus
w/ Bass Fig. 1

I'm so ti - red I can't sleep. _____

I'm a li - ar and a thief. _____

I sit and drink ___ Pen - ny Roy - al Tea. _____

I'm a ne - mic roy - al - ty. _____

Interlude

D.S. al Coda

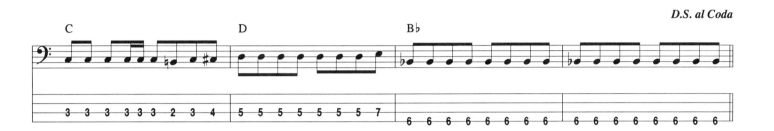

⊕ *Coda*

Outro

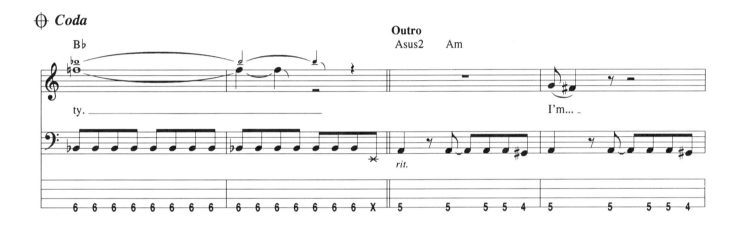

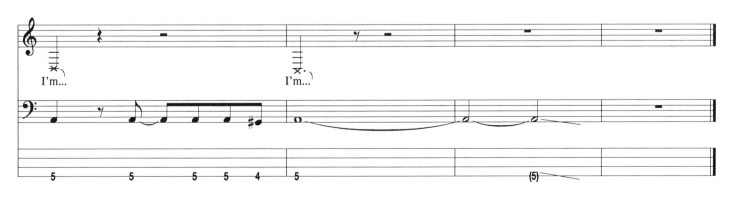

(New Wave) Polly

Words and Music by Kurt Cobain

Tune Down 1/2 Step:
②= Gb ③= Ab
①= Db ④= Eb

Intro
Moderately ♩ = 120

𝄋 Verse

w/ Bass Fig. 2, (mf) 2 times, 2nd & 3rd times

1. Pol - ly wants a crack - er,
2. Pol - ly wants a crack - er,
3. Pol - ly says her back ___ hurts,

I think I should get off ___ her first. ___ I think she wants some
may - be she would like ___ more food. ___ Asks me to un -
and she's just ___ as bored ___ as me. ___ She caught ___ me

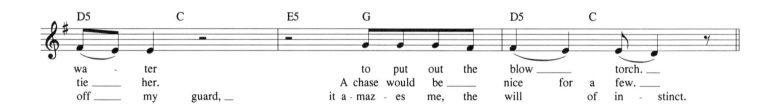

wa - ter   to put out the blow ___ torch. ___
tie ___ her.   A chase would be ___ nice for a few. ___
off ___ my guard, ___   it a - maz - es me, the will of in - stinct.

Chorus

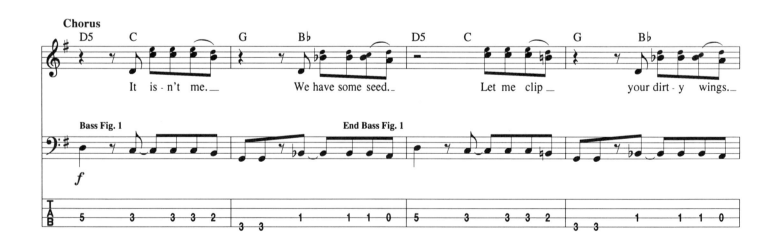

It is - n't me. ___   We have some seed. ___   Let me clip ___   your dirt - y wings. ___

Bass Fig. 1   **End Bass Fig. 1**

w/ Bass Fig. 1, 6 times, simile

Let me take a ride. _ Don't hurt your-self. _ I want some help, _ to help my-self. _

I've got some rope, _ you have been told. _ I prom-ise you _ I have been true. _

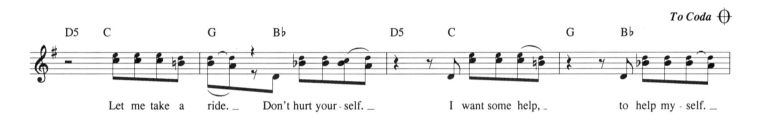

To Coda ⊕

Let me take a ride. _ Don't hurt your-self. _ I want some help, _ to help my-self. _

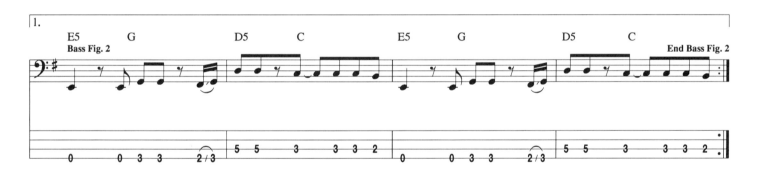

Bass Fig. 2 ... End Bass Fig. 2

D.S. al Coda

Pol-ly said.

⊕ *Coda*

Rape Me

Words and Music by Kurt Cobain

Tune Down 1/2 Step:
②= Gb ③= Ab
①= Db ④= Eb

Intro
Moderate Rock ♩ = 110

Bass tacet

Verse

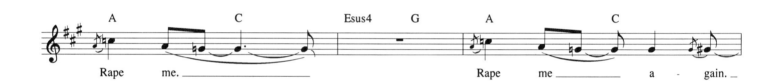

1. Rape me. ___ Rape me, ___ my friend. ___

Rape me. ___ Rape me a - gain. ___

Chorus

I'm not the on - ly one. ___ I, ___ I'm not the on - ly one. ___ I, ___

w/ Bass Fig. 1

I'm not the on - ly one. ___ I, ___ I'm not the on - ly one. ___

Verse

w/ Bass Fig. 1, 2 times

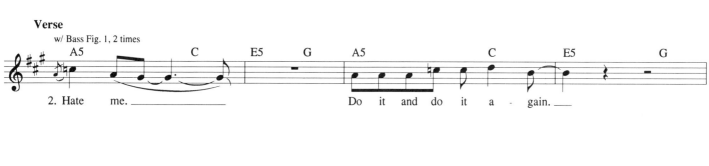

2. Hate me. Do it and do it a-gain.

Waste me. Taste me, my friend.

Chorus

w/ Bass Fig. 1, 2 times

I'm not the on - ly one. I, I'm not the on - ly one. I,

I'm not the on - ly one. I, I'm not the on - ly one.

Bridge

My fav-'rite in-side source. I'll kiss your o - pen sores.

Ap-pre-ci-ate your con-cern. You'll al-ways stink and burn.

Verse

Bass tacet

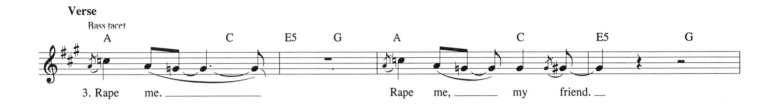

3. Rape me. _____ Rape me, _____ my friend. _____

w/ Bass Fill 1

Rape me. _____ Rape me, _____ a - gain. _____

Chorus

w/ Bass Fig. 1, 2 times

I'm not the on - ly one. _____ I, _____ I'm not the on - ly one. _____ I, _____

I'm not the on - ly one. _____ I, _____ I'm not the on - ly one. _____

Free Time

play 4 times

Rape me. _____ Rape me. _____ Rape me. _____
Rape me. _____ Rape me. _____

Smells Like Teen Spirit

Words and Music by Kurt Cobain, Chris Novoselic and David Grohl

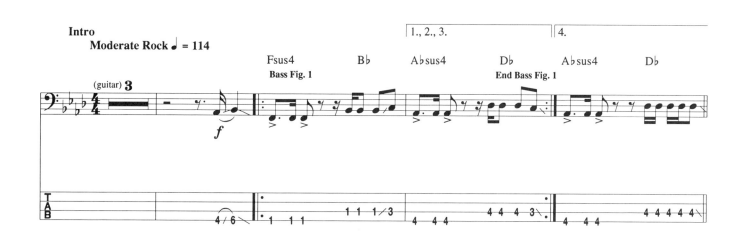

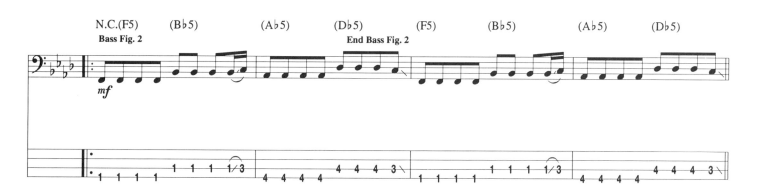

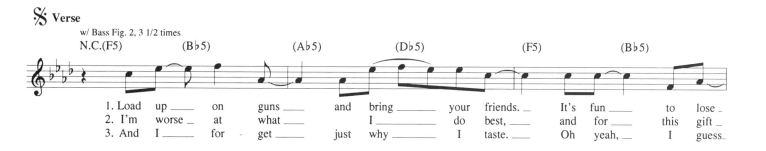

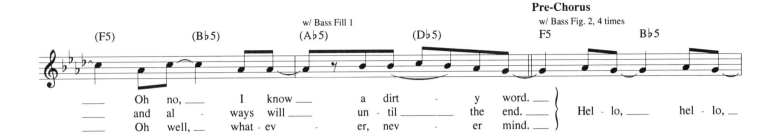

Pre-Chorus
w/ Bass Fig. 2, 4 times

(F5) (Bb5) w/ Bass Fill 1 (Ab5) (Db5) F5 Bb5

_____ Oh no, _____ I know _____ a dirt - y word. _____
_____ and al - ways will _____ un - til _____ the end. _____ Hel - lo, _____ hel - lo, _____
_____ Oh well, _____ what - ev - er, nev - er mind. _____

Ab5 Db5 F5 Bb5 Ab5 Db5 F5 Bb5

_____ hel - lo, _____ how _ low? _____ Hel - lo, _____ hel - lo, _____ hel - lo, _____ how _ low? _____ Hel - lo, _____ hel - lo, _

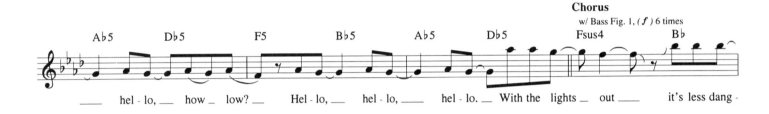

Chorus
w/ Bass Fig. 1, (*f*) 6 times

Ab5 Db5 F5 Bb5 Ab5 Db5 Fsus4 Bb

_____ hel - lo, _____ how _ low? _____ Hel - lo, _____ hel - lo, _____ hel - lo. _ With the lights _ out _____ it's less dang -

Absus4 Db Fsus4 Bb Absus4 Db Fsus4 Bb

- 'rous. Here we are _____ now, en - ter - tain _____ us. I feel stu - pid _____ and con - ta -

Absus4 Db Fsus4 Bb Absus4 Db Fsus4 Bb

- gious. Here we are _____ now, en - ter - tain _____ us. A mul - la - to, _____ an al - bi -

Bass Fill 1

52

Stain

Words and Music by Kurt Cobain

Drop D Tuning:
①=G ③=A
②=D ④=D

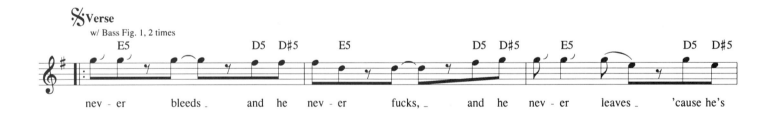

nev - er bleeds ___ and he nev - er fucks, ___ and he nev - er leaves ___ 'cause he's

got bad luck. Well he nev - er reads ___ and he nev - er roughs, ___ and he

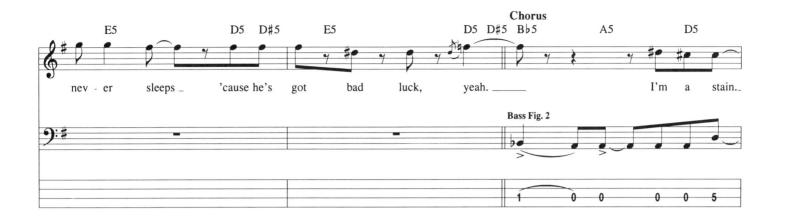

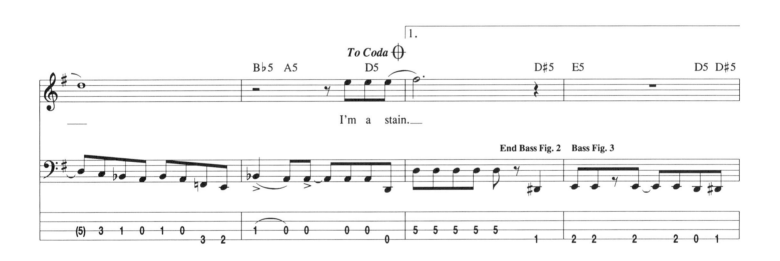

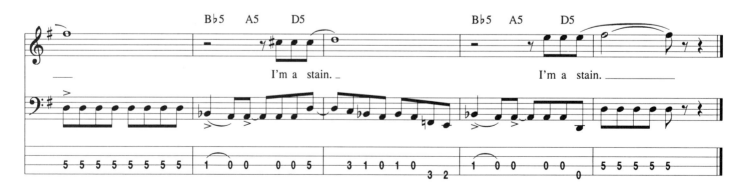

Stay Away

Words and Music by Kurt Cobain

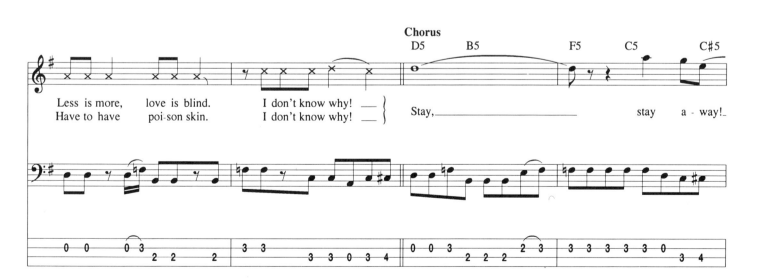

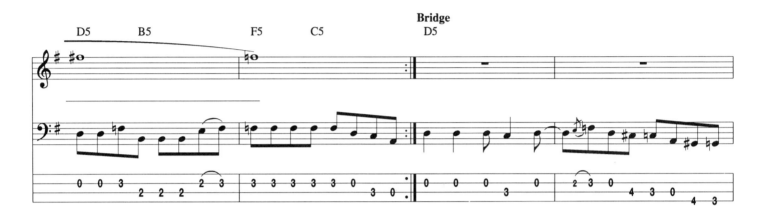

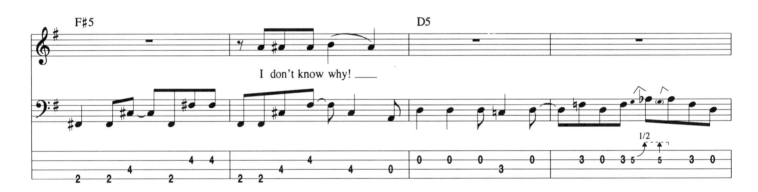

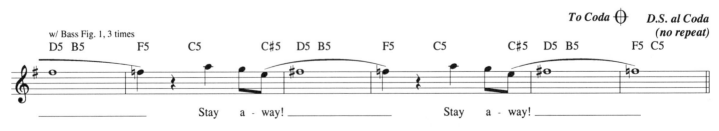

⊕ Coda

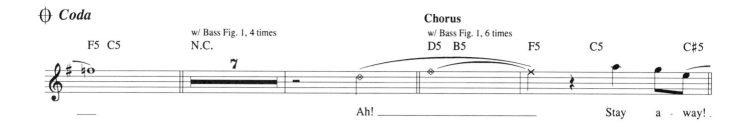

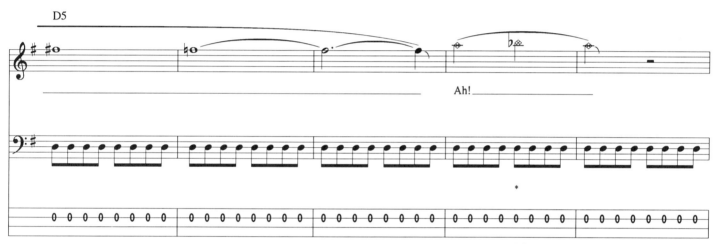

* Gradually detune tuning peg till end.

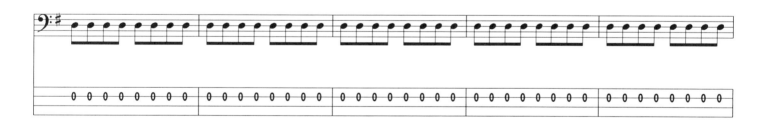

Free Time

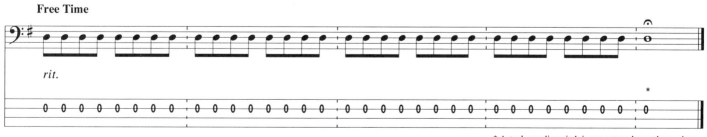

* Actual sounding pitch is one octave lower than written.

Bass Notation Legend

Bass music can be notated two different ways: on a *musical staff*, and in *tablature*.

THE MUSICAL STAFF shows pitches and rhythms and is divided by bar lines into measures. Pitches are named after the first seven letters of the alphabet.

TABLATURE graphically represents the bass fingerboard. Each horizontal line represents a string, and each number represents a fret.

3rd string, open   2nd string, 2nd fret   1st & 2nd strings open, played together

HAMMER-ON: Strike the first (lower) note with one finger, then sound the higher note (on the same string) with another finger by fretting it without picking.

PULL-OFF: Place both fingers on the notes to be sounded. Strike the first note and without picking, pull the finger off to sound the second (lower) note.

LEGATO SLIDE: Strike the first note and then slide the same fret-hand finger up or down to the second note. The second note is not struck.

SHIFT SLIDE: Same as legato slide, except the second note is struck.

TRILL: Very rapidly alternate between the notes indicated by continuously hammering on and pulling off.

TREMOLO PICKING: The note is picked as rapidly and continuously as possible.

VIBRATO: The string is vibrated by rapidly bending and releasing the note with the fretting hand.

SHAKE: Using one finger, rapidly alternate between two notes on one string by sliding either a half-step above or below.

NATURAL HARMONIC: Strike the note while the fret hand lightly touches the string directly over the fret indicated.

MUFFLED STRINGS: A percussive sound is produced by laying the fret hand across the string(s) without depressing them and striking them with the pick hand.

BEND: Strike the note and bend up the interval shown.

BEND AND RELEASE: Strike the note and bend up as indicated, then release back to the original note. Only the first note is struck.

RIGHT-HAND TAP: Hammer ("tap") the fret indicated with the "pick-hand" index or middle finger and pull off to the note fretted by the fret hand.

LEFT-HAND TAP: Hammer ("tap") the fret indicated with the "fret-hand" index or middle finger.

SLAP: Strike ("slap") string with right-hand thumb.

POP: Snap ("pop") string with right-hand index or middle finger.

Additional Musical Definitions

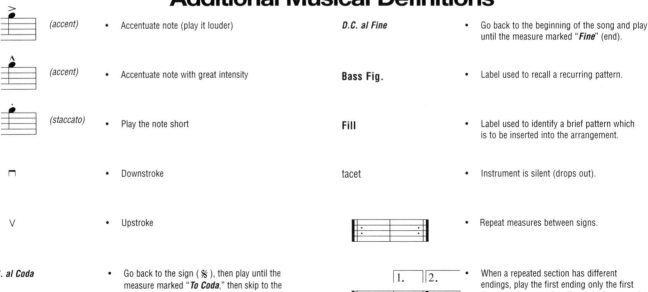

(accent)	•	Accentuate note (play it louder)
(accent)	•	Accentuate note with great intensity
(staccato)	•	Play the note short
⊓	•	Downstroke
V	•	Upstroke

D.S. al Coda   • Go back to the sign (𝄋), then play until the measure marked "*To Coda*," then skip to the section labelled "*Coda*."

D.C. al Fine   • Go back to the beginning of the song and play until the measure marked "*Fine*" (end).

Bass Fig.   • Label used to recall a recurring pattern.

Fill   • Label used to identify a brief pattern which is to be inserted into the arrangement.

tacet   • Instrument is silent (drops out).

   • Repeat measures between signs.

• When a repeated section has different endings, play the first ending only the first time and the second ending only the second time.

NOTE: Tablature numbers in parentheses mean:
1. The note is being sustained over a system (note in standard notation is tied), or
2. The note is sustained, but a new articulation (such as a hammer-on, pull-off, slide or vibrato begins, or
3. The note is a barely audible "ghost" note (note in standard notation is also in parentheses).